CHANEL BLACKMORE

*Key Strategies for Female
Entrepreneurs to Move You
from Stuck to Bossing Up!*

WATCH ME *werk!*

STAND IN YOUR POWER

Printed in the United States of America

ISBN-13: 9781729477847

Contents

Other books by Author Chanel Blackmore:

What's in Your Box?

The Identity Thief: 21-Day Devotional

www.justbmore.com

Polish Your Purpose

> "*You are the most influential person you will talk to all day.*"
> -Zig Ziggler

I would like to start by sharing my story with you. I'm not your typical business owner. In the beginning of my journey into entrepreneurship, I had no clue what I wanted to do. I didn't know really what I *liked* to do. I didn't know who I was or where my passion lay. I just knew I was sick of going to work day in and day out. I knew I was tired of living paycheck to paycheck; just barely getting by. I was so over it!

So what's a girl to do when she's sick and tired of being SICK AND TIRED? I started searching on the internet for business opportunities. My first venture into entrepreneurship was making baskets for weddings and baby showers. I was really good at it! I made dozens of beautiful baskets and had a steady flow of customers. I earned a good profit, but I didn't have any repeat customers. During that time, my knowledge of marketing was very limited and for that reason, my business failed.

My next venture was with a Multi-Level Marketing (MLM) company. I went to one of those meetings and heard the presentation; I was sold on the buy-in immediately. I had home parties and dazzled my hostesses. My calendar was booked due to word of mouth, but I noticed that I was only earning a very small percentage of what I sold. I also realized that I was working way too hard to earn it!

I tried many other ventures and found that I just couldn't stay with it long enough to make the money I needed to change my situation.

It wasn't long before I began to think that I may not be cut out for business ownership. I thought that I should focus on getting an education or climbing the corporate ladder. I felt utterly defeated and stuck.

I was just about to give up and I had resolved to focus on my career instead of entrepreneurship. I'd decided that I was through with businesses both traditional and MLM.

Just when I thought I was done, I had an interesting conversation with my friend's husband. He asked me a simple question, "Chanel, what do you have in your hand?"

Of course, I was floored. Essentially, he was pointing out that my gifts should be the source of my business. That blew my mind!

He went on to explain that my business and my passion was connected. It was <u>then</u> that I found my purpose.

> *"Some entrepreneurs think how can I make a lot of money? But the better way is to think, how can I make people's lives a lot better? If you get it right, the money will come."*
> -Richard Branson

I cannot stress the importance of PASSION and PURPOSE. You have to do a personal inventory of your gifts and your passion. This is done by asking the following questions:

1. What do you really want out of life? This will help you clearly identify and define what you care about.

2. If all of your problems (money, time) were resolved, what would you do?

3. In what things are you most interested?

4. What skills come to you naturally?

5. What activities do you lose yourself in when you're involved? Meaning you totally lose track of time because you are so engulfed in that activity.

Within the answers to these questions, you will find your passion. Once your passion is identified, your purpose becomes clear!

> "If you want to be successful in this world, you have to follow your passion, not a paycheck."
> -Jen Welter

Trust me, it is impossible to find peace in your business if you are not passionate about what you are doing. Passion will be the thing that keeps you focused on your goal. Passion is what will keep you moving and executing. Without it, you will not last.

When you have a vision for your life, it gives you clarity. Clarity is very important. Clarity helps you hone in on your target market and identify HOW you will serve them.

You see, when you know what you're supposed to be doing, it helps you carve out your niche. That's a hard thing to do if you lack vision, focus, and passion.

I hear you! You're asking, "How do I find my purpose?"

Here are some targeted questions to help you out:

1. What problems do you want to solve?

2. What role would you like to play in resolving the problem?

3. What skills do you have that will impact the problem?

4. Would you solve the problem for FREE if you had to?

These simple questions will help you identify your purpose. Once you have that, you can begin to move towards your destiny.

You Have to BOSS UP!

> "No amount of security is worth the suffering of a mediocre life chained to a routine that has killed your dreams."
> -Maya Mendoza

In order to run a successful business, you have to Boss Up! Entrepreneurship is not for the WEAK. You have to be able to handle rejection, criticism, and disappointments.

Bossing up means that you have to own your business. You have to treat it like a real business. NOT a Hobby!

Most entrepreneurs fail at this. They fail because of two major reasons. One, they treat their business as if it is not valuable. They won't charge their worth, they are practically giving their gifts away for free.

Secondly, they invest more time to their corporate jobs than they do to something that will set them financially free. This is a huge mistake!

If you are going to be successful in business, you have to invest time, money, and energy. It means nothing to start a business and then leave it alone. It would be like a woman giving birth and leaving her child to fend for itself. Horrible right?

How can you expect a business to thrive when there is no one minding the store?

I remember my business venture with that MLM company I told you about earlier; and I just KNEW I was going to get rich. I signed up, paid my money, and waited. No support came from my up line. No one taught me how to grow it. It just sat there, going nowhere.

I realized really quickly that without help, my business would fail. And it DID. It's not enough to want to be in business, you have to BE in BUSINESS. This means learning about your industry; building relationships and investing in personal and professional development.

It also means taking total ownership of the business. You can't wait on anyone else to nurture and grow your business.

You have to do it. You also have to realize that no one is coming to save you. I know this is supposed to be a motivational book, but I have to tell you the truth. Straight up, no chaser. You have to be accountable for what takes place in your business. How do you do that?

1. **INVEST TIME.** Set aside time to cast a vision for your business. Where do you want to go? Who do you want to serve? How much money do you want to make? Begin answering these questions and you can chart a successful course.

2. **INVEST MONEY.** Please don't think that you are going to grow a business without investing your own money. Invest in branding and marketing. Don't try to do everything yourself. Be

smart. People will buy what looks professional.

3. **TAKE AN HONEST ASSESSMENT.** Inspect what you expect. If your business isn't making a profit, you must take a hard look at it and determine the problem.

Bosses Stay Slayed Up and Prayed Up

> "Faith is required if you are going to upgrade from rickety to rolling in it because faith is the part of us that dares to believe that an unseen, unproven, {and often proven otherwise} brand new and awesome reality is in our grasp."
> -Jen Sincero

Faith is a HUGE part of business. It takes faith to come up with a vision. Listen, it's been said that if your vision doesn't scare you, it's not big enough. This is true. You must know that in order to live big, you have to dream BIG!

The amount of faith that you have directly correlates to how far you will go and how successful you will be. I don't want you to start rolling your eyes and saying, "Here we go with the God thing," however, faith is important.

When you decided to go into business, that took faith. Faith is simply believing in something that has not appeared or manifested yet. Think about it. God spoke the world into existence from a thought. Wait, let me explain.

You see, when the Lord said, "Let there be light," it was dark y'all, there was NO light!

You have the same power. You have to understand that God used faith to create this world. He didn't SEE anything to create SOMETHING. What does this have to do with business? EVERYTHING!

All that you see in this world came from an idea. It was an idea that someone imagined and invested time, money and energy to create. That's a huge part of what business is. It's taking a God-given idea and trusting Him enough to make it happen.

Many of us have great ideas but no faith. We sit with pen and paper, writing and jotting down any and everything that comes to our minds, but we don't do anything with it. We fail to trust not only in our gifts, but the One who is the gift giver.

I submit to you that the God we serve gives us ideas to create wealth in this world. Now listen, wealth is not just money and material things. For example, if you have a sick family member, and they need medical attention, love won't take care of it. You will need money.

Additionally, if you need to be by that person's bedside, a corporate job won't always allow you to do that. You have to be financially secure.

I get it. The faith thing has been abused and overused. Trust me, you have to have faith in something greater than yourself to take this journey into entrepreneurship. This is a trip you cannot afford to take alone.

Faith will keep you focused on what God whispered to you in prayer. Faith will help you block out the voices of your haters. Faith will keep your feet moving when you want to quit. You see, faith is the thing that we believe and have not seen. Without it, you won't go very far in your business.

> "You don't start a business with an idea, you start with God through prayer."
> -Jerry J. Panou

I hear you asking, "Why is prayer important?" Listen, I know that not everyone prays. I get it. However, I'm telling you this story from my perspective. I truly believe that I would not have been as successful as I am today if I had not prayed about decisions before making them. Prayer is important for several reasons:

1. You must pray for WISDOM. Wisdom is going to be very important especially if you have never owned a business before. You will need to ask for wisdom when applying for a loan or financial support. Wisdom is needed when hiring employees.

2. You need to pray for CREATIVITY. There's nothing like divine inspiration. I receive the best ideas while in prayer.

3. You need to pray for a HEALTHY IDENTITY. In any type of business, knowing who you are is paramount! It's so easy to launch a business and lose yourself in it or in what others think it should be. Prayer will keep you

focused on who God is thereby keeping you focused on who you are.

4. You need to pray for the <u>right</u> PARTNERS, INVESTORS, and CONNECTIONS.

You also have to trust in your ability to make it happen. That's faith! Prayer plus faith equals results.

I wish I could tell you that faith and prayer alone works, but I'd be lying to you. It is the faith that will push you to execute your ideas. If you believe in it, you will work towards it.

Let me repeat that... if you believe in IT, you will work towards IT. No one can believe for you. This is your creation, you have to trust in what you imagined. You have to love it first. How can you come up with an idea that you don't believe in and expect it to prosper? That doesn't make sense. You have to believe. When others see you working faithfully towards your vision, they will come and join you in the journey.

Werk, Werk, Werk, WERK

> "I'd rather be tired than **broke**."
> -Kevin Heart

Along with faith, you need a strong work ethic. In order to do anything in this world, there must be work involved. You can't expect to do great things when you are not willing to put in the necessary effort to bring it to pass.

One of the most important aspects of business is execution. No, not death by firing squad, but taking a plan and moving it towards completion.

How can you say you want financial freedom or that you are a BOSS and NOT put forth the action required? Now that's a question worth considering.

It's like purchasing a new car and never taking it to be insured or registered. You simply purchased something you cannot drive! You can have a great concept for a business, but if you don't develop it or take the steps to grow it, it won't move.

It's a process! I know many of us hate THAT word, but it is a huge part of life. Let me ask you a question: How many people do you know that have had children?

When a woman is pregnant, she starts preparing immediately. She selects the room in which the baby will sleep. She packs her bags to include things she will need while in the hospital. She starts picking out names for her child. Come on, you know the drill. This is part of the child rearing process.

Building a business is the same way. You have to start implementing things that will grow your business. You cannot depend on *luck* to do it.

> "You can't have a million dollar dream with a minimum wage work ethic."
> -Stephen C. Hogan

Mediocre effort will yield mediocre results. I'll let that one sink in…

If you don't invest the work needed to grow your business, you may as well quit now. Here's another question: Why do many of us go to a corporate job that we hate?

The job pays us less than what we are worth however we give 110%? We stay late, come in early, and skip lunch. We sit in endless meetings, miss our children's important events, and work while on vacation.

Why? Is it because we hope to receive something? A promotion? Recognition? What?!

Most of the time, we don't even get a pat on the back. However, we still go in early, stay late… Well you know the rest. Now when you start a business, YOUR business, you only spend an hour or so a day working it.

It's okay, just say "OUCH"!

You pour so much of your time and energy into your job, you don't have any left for your business.

If you are working a job, I want you to pay special attention right here. You may be a manager at your job, or a Vice President. You are expected to work longer, harder, and not use your vacation time.

You are told if you work harder, you will reap the benefits. Let's say you make $75,000 annually. Your boss makes $120,000 and his or her boss makes

$225,000 annually. What I want you to know is that the OWNER is making millions!

Now don't get me wrong, the aforementioned salaries are great. However, the owner is making all of the money. The owner of the company is building a legacy for his or her children while you work! If you want true financial freedom, you have to do the work.

I've heard many excuses as to why it can't be done. Why you can't spend the time needed to grow your business. Your business is the vehicle that will build a legacy for your children and their children. Your business is the key to you leaving your job. The key to financial freedom, but you won't work it. You continue to drag your feet and months and years pass with no success.

I'll tell you this, your business didn't fail; you failed your business. It's a hard truth but until you face it and deal with it, nothing you launch will succeed.

I think the best way to handle this is to focus on the type of lifestyle you want. It's like the Word of God says, "See the end from the beginning."

Imagine your life without a job. See yourself free of bosses, meetings, limited lunch breaks, and vacations. Picture your children's college education paid for in cash. Envision you and your family taking vacations and trips. Think of all of this without having to worry about where the money is coming from! That's true financial freedom.

Boss Ladies Play

> "Some women fear the fire. Some women simply become it."
> -R.H. Sin

Now that you know a strong, consistent work ethic is a MUST in business, you need to slay it. What does that mean?

In every aspect of your business, you should be dominating. Execution is key. What good is a plan when you have no follow through? You can't expect your business to work if you don't. It's one thing to write down a plan and create vision board, but it's another to make it happen.

Creating a vision board or goals is just the first step. Execution is making sure you are consistently completing those tasks that will continue to move your business forward.

Here are a few tips to ensure that you are executing in your business:

1. **WRITE DOWN YOUR PLANS.** The Bible tells us to write the vision and make it plain. It also says in another scripture that without a vision, the people perish. This just means that you can't drive your business if you don't know where it's going. Who determines this? You do! You have to create a clear, concise vision for your business. How can you dominate something that is

aimless? Ideas are great to start with, however, you must clarify your focus. You must hone in on the direction you want to go.

2. **NEXT, YOU WANT TO BREAK YOUR PLANS DOWN INTO SMALL MEASURABLE GOALS.** For example, if you are planning a huge launch, you must include deadlines and targets. Remember, we are aiming for something. It's easier to aim at a small target than the entire wall. I'm reminded of snipers in the military (sorry I LOVE Call of Duty). Snipers don't shoot haphazardly at the enemy. They focus in on a specific target and FIRE! You need to have that kind of precision in your business.

3. **NOW MOVE**! You have to accomplish those goals. This is going to require the

work ethic that we discussed earlier. You have to drive towards these goals keeping the end in mind.

4. **EXECUTE RELENTLESSLY**! Don't skip any steps or cut any corners. Remember this is YOUR baby. Give it the attention it needs to grow so it can take care of you one day.

Making Money Moves!

"Your mind will believe whatever you continuously tell it. So tell it you are smart, ambitious, cute, and not afraid to go for it."
-BossBabeQuote

How do you make money moves? By honing in on your desires and goals. It's easy to say that you want to be an entrepreneur, but do you really?

It's also easy to say that you want to achieve a lifestyle that is debt free and full of financial freedom. But how bad do you want it?

This is where your natural drive to succeed comes into play. Some will call it, ambition. What is ambition? Ambition is defined as a strong desire to do or to achieve something, typically requiring determination and hard work.

Why do you need it? Ambition will show you how bad you really want it. I know that ambition or being ambitious gets a bad rap, but I have to say that without it NOTHING gets done!

What if you don't have ambition? How do you develop the ambition you currently possess?

1. **YOU HAVE TO SET GOALS**. Remember this is KEY. You have to set a course in

place. It's like driving around a city with no destination in mind.

2. **YOU HAVE TO LEARN TO TAKE RISKS.** Do not let fear hinder your movement. If you become stuck in fear, you will never accomplish your dream and your business will perish.

3. **YOU HAVE TO BE OPEN MINDED.** Yes, you have to be open to new ways of thinking as well as new ideas. Just because one thing worked for someone else doesn't mean it will work for you. You have to be open to trying everything until you find the one that works for you.

4. **YOU HAVE TO EXECUTE RELENTLESSLY!** Yes, I'm saying it again! You have to focus on getting things done.

5. **YOU HAVE TO SURROUND YOURSELF WITH OTHER AMBITION PEOPLE.** Ambition is contagious. You have to increase your circle to include others that are like-minded regarding business. The more you hang around hungry people, suddenly, you become hungry. Make sense?

At the end of the day, you have to ask yourself, "How bad do I want this?" Then, you must ask, "How hard am I willing to work to get it?"

Boss Ladies Know Who They Are

> "Me? Princess? No honey. I don't think so.
> I'm the Queen."
> -Anonymous

Now let's work on your value system. None of the things I mentioned before will work if you don't know your value and worth.

You have to understand that nothing in this world will be given to you. You must also know that no one will value you if you don't demand it. You have to believe that you are worthy of happiness, love, and wealth. I know that sounds strange, but you simply MUST.

It doesn't matter what business you launch or if you decide to be an author. If you don't know your worth, you will be under paid and undervalued.

This will inevitably cause you to give up and quit. People will only pay you based on how you see yourself. Don't forget your business is a reflection of you. This all goes back to how you see yourself and how you assess your own value. I can't stress how important this is!

In order for you to slay in business, you have to know who you are. You have to love who you are. It all starts with YOU!

Many of us have never had anyone tell us positive things. We've put everyone and everything before our dreams. We have sacrificed and settled in so many areas of our lives. Well I say, enough is enough!

It's time to get up and Boss Up! It's time to dominate life. Yes! Let's start by believing that we deserve a better lifestyle. Let's begin to tell ourselves that we earned the right to be Bosses in every way.

Come on now, it starts with you! Remember that. It starts with how you see yourself and how you talk to yourself.

Oh, you think you don't talk to yourself? Every time you try something different, you talk yourself out of it. You say things like, "I really don't need this." Or "this costs too much." I definitely can relate.

Negative self-talk will KILL your dreams and stagnation in your life. I want you to be successful. I want you to be great. You have to know that there is greatness deep down inside of you. You have to not only believe it, you have to KNOW! You have to take hold of this idea that you are destined for greatness. That you have a purpose in life that only you can fulfill.

It's cool, I get it. We as women were never taught to take care of ourselves. We grew up being taught how to cook, clean, have children… Yeah, I know.

As little girls, we were groomed to be great wives, and loving mothers. And there is nothing wrong with that! However, I do believe that you can have more; that you can BE more.

Now, if you don't want more, no worries, I'm not talking to you. I'm talking to the women who are tired of going to a job where they are underpaid, undervalued, and limited. I'm talking to those who have dreams, goals, and ideas. I'm telling you that you can be great! You can have more! You can be more if you so desire it.

I want to help you in this. Remember, if you don't have confidence, you will struggle to make the kind of money you want. Here are some affirmations that will get you started:

1. Today, I will take my life to the next level.

2. I choose to believe in myself and my ability.

3. I am created in the image of God and I have all that I need to succeed.

4. Today, I choose to believe in my own destiny and that I have purpose.

5. I am smart, funny, and gifted.

6. My gifts will make room for me.

7. I have talents to share with the world and the world will pay me for them.

8. Today, I choose to cancel every curse that was spoken over my life that was meant to keep me stuck in fear.

9. I am confident, strong, and qualified to do what I'm purposed.

10. I'm the only one who can stop me from being successful.

In closing, I want to encourage you to go for it! Dream harder, work longer, strive for excellence.

I know that you've heard these things before. Most often, referencing a career or job.

However, I want you to do these things for YOU. Build a legacy for your children and their children. Launch a family business, one that can guarantee generational wealth.

It's possible and I promise you, in the end, it's WORTH IT!

~ THE END ~

Made in the USA
Columbia, SC
19 November 2024